THIS JOURNAL BELONGS TO

_____

THE
FISHERMAN'S
JOURNAL

HOW TO USE THIS BOOK

WELCOME TO YOUR JOURNAL, a place to reflect on your best (and worst) fishing experiences, take notes for the future, and keep track of your most epic catches.

This book is divided into three parts. The first, Fishing Logs, is the heart of the book. Here, you have a place to record details about every time you go fishing, allowing you to keep track of your favorite spots, the conditions you've experienced, and all the details about what worked and what didn't. Each log has a page with blank spaces for key information about the location, the weather, and the fish you caught, plus a lined page you can use for additional notes. At the beginning of the section, you'll find a DIY index where you can enter the location and date for each log entry as you work through the journal.

Following the fishing logs, there's a section with blank pages where you can include any extra notes and sketches—map your favorite fishing hole, keep running equipment lists, or just reminisce about a great day out on the water. The final section, Fishing Lists, gives you a place to list your favorite fishing trips, your fishing bucket list, and all the types of fish you've caught (so far).

HAPPY FISHING!

FISHING LOGS

FISHING LOG INDEX

LOG #	LOCATION	DATE

LOG #	LOCATION	DATE

FISHING LOG INDEX

LOG #	LOCATION	DATE

LOG #	LOCATION	DATE

FISHING LOG

LOG #

DATE

FISHING COMPANIONS

LOCATION

OBSERVATIONS

HIGHLIGHTS

WEATHER _____ **MOON PHASE** _____

AIR TEMPERATURE _____ **WATER TEMPERATURE** _____

WIND SPEED/DIRECTION _____

WATER CONDITIONS (level, clarity) _____

EQUIPMENT USED _____

CATCHLIST				
SPECIES	LENGTH / WEIGHT	BAIT/LURE/FLY	OTHER TACKLE	TIME

OVERALL RATING

FISHING LOG

LOG #

DATE

FISHING COMPANIONS

LOCATION

OBSERVATIONS

HIGHLIGHTS

WEATHER _____ MOON PHASE _____

AIR TEMPERATURE _____ WATER TEMPERATURE _____

WIND SPEED/DIRECTION _____

WATER CONDITIONS (level, clarity) _____

EQUIPMENT USED _____

CATCHLIST				
SPECIES	LENGTH / WEIGHT	BAIT/LURE/FLY	OTHER TACKLE	TIME

OVERALL RATING

FISHING LOG

LOG #

DATE

FISHING COMPANIONS

LOCATION

OBSERVATIONS _____

_____
_____
_____
_____
_____
_____
_____
_____
_____
_____
_____
_____
_____
_____
_____
_____
_____
_____

HIGHLIGHTS _____

_____
_____
_____

WEATHER _____ MOON PHASE _____

AIR TEMPERATURE _____ WATER TEMPERATURE _____

WIND SPEED/DIRECTION _____

WATER CONDITIONS (level, clarity) _____

EQUIPMENT USED _____

CATCHLIST				
SPECIES	LENGTH / WEIGHT	BAIT/LURE/FLY	OTHER TACKLE	TIME

OVERALL RATING

FISHING LOG

LOG #

DATE

FISHING COMPANIONS

LOCATION

OBSERVATIONS

HIGHLIGHTS

WEATHER _____ **MOON PHASE** _____

AIR TEMPERATURE _____ **WATER TEMPERATURE** _____

WIND SPEED/DIRECTION _____

WATER CONDITIONS (level, clarity) _____

EQUIPMENT USED _____

CATCHLIST				
SPECIES	LENGTH / WEIGHT	BAIT/LURE/FLY	OTHER TACKLE	TIME

OVERALL RATING

FISHING LOG

LOG #

DATE

FISHING COMPANIONS

LOCATION

OBSERVATIONS

HIGHLIGHTS

WEATHER _____ **MOON PHASE** _____

AIR TEMPERATURE _____ **WATER TEMPERATURE** _____

WIND SPEED/DIRECTION _____

WATER CONDITIONS (level, clarity) _____

EQUIPMENT USED _____

CATCHLIST				
SPECIES	LENGTH / WEIGHT	BAIT/LURE/FLY	OTHER TACKLE	TIME

OVERALL RATING

FISHING LOG

LOG #

DATE

FISHING COMPANIONS

LOCATION

OBSERVATIONS _____

_____

_____

_____

_____

_____

_____

_____

_____

_____

_____

_____

_____

_____

_____

_____

_____

_____

_____

_____

_____

HIGHLIGHTS _____

_____

_____

_____

WEATHER _____ MOON PHASE _____

AIR TEMPERATURE _____ WATER TEMPERATURE _____

WIND SPEED/DIRECTION _____

WATER CONDITIONS (level, clarity) _____

EQUIPMENT USED _____

CATCHLIST				
SPECIES	LENGTH / WEIGHT	BAIT/LURE/FLY	OTHER TACKLE	TIME

OVERALL RATING ▶🐟 ▶🐟 ▶🐟 ▶🐟 ▶🐟

FISHING LOG

LOG #

DATE

FISHING COMPANIONS

LOCATION

OBSERVATIONS

HIGHLIGHTS

WEATHER _____ MOON PHASE _____

AIR TEMPERATURE _____ WATER TEMPERATURE _____

WIND SPEED/DIRECTION _____

WATER CONDITIONS (level, clarity) _____

EQUIPMENT USED _____

CATCHLIST				
SPECIES	LENGTH / WEIGHT	BAIT/LURE/FLY	OTHER TACKLE	TIME

OVERALL RATING

FISHING LOG

LOG #

DATE

FISHING COMPANIONS

LOCATION

OBSERVATIONS

HIGHLIGHTS

WEATHER _____ MOON PHASE _____

AIR TEMPERATURE _____ WATER TEMPERATURE _____

WIND SPEED/DIRECTION _____

WATER CONDITIONS (level, clarity) _____

EQUIPMENT USED _____

CATCHLIST				
SPECIES	LENGTH / WEIGHT	BAIT/LURE/FLY	OTHER TACKLE	TIME

OVERALL RATING

FISHING LOG

LOG #

DATE

FISHING COMPANIONS

LOCATION

OBSERVATIONS

HIGHLIGHTS

WEATHER _____ **MOON PHASE** _____

AIR TEMPERATURE _____ **WATER TEMPERATURE** _____

WIND SPEED/DIRECTION _____

WATER CONDITIONS (level, clarity) _____

EQUIPMENT USED _____

CATCHLIST				
SPECIES	LENGTH / WEIGHT	BAIT/LURE/FLY	OTHER TACKLE	TIME

OVERALL RATING

FISHING LOG

LOG #

DATE

FISHING COMPANIONS

LOCATION

OBSERVATIONS

HIGHLIGHTS

WEATHER _____ **MOON PHASE** _____

AIR TEMPERATURE _____ **WATER TEMPERATURE** _____

WIND SPEED/DIRECTION _____

WATER CONDITIONS (level, clarity) _____

EQUIPMENT USED _____

CATCHLIST				
SPECIES	LENGTH / WEIGHT	BAIT/LURE/FLY	OTHER TACKLE	TIME

OVERALL RATING

FISHING LOG

LOG #

DATE

FISHING COMPANIONS

LOCATION

OBSERVATIONS

HIGHLIGHTS

WEATHER _____   MOON PHASE _____

AIR TEMPERATURE _____   WATER TEMPERATURE _____

WIND SPEED/DIRECTION _____

WATER CONDITIONS (level, clarity) _____

EQUIPMENT USED _____

CATCHLIST				
SPECIES	LENGTH / WEIGHT	BAIT/LURE/FLY	OTHER TACKLE	TIME

OVERALL RATING

FISHING LOG

LOG #

DATE

FISHING COMPANIONS

LOCATION

OBSERVATIONS

HIGHLIGHTS

WEATHER _____ **MOON PHASE** _____

AIR TEMPERATURE _____ **WATER TEMPERATURE** _____

WIND SPEED/DIRECTION _____

WATER CONDITIONS (level, clarity) _____

EQUIPMENT USED _____

CATCHLIST				
SPECIES	LENGTH / WEIGHT	BAIT/LURE/FLY	OTHER TACKLE	TIME

OVERALL RATING

FISHING LOG

LOG #

DATE

FISHING COMPANIONS

LOCATION

OBSERVATIONS

HIGHLIGHTS

WEATHER _____ MOON PHASE _____

AIR TEMPERATURE _____ WATER TEMPERATURE _____

WIND SPEED/DIRECTION _____

WATER CONDITIONS (level, clarity) _____

EQUIPMENT USED _____

CATCHLIST				
SPECIES	LENGTH / WEIGHT	BAIT/LURE/FLY	OTHER TACKLE	TIME

OVERALL RATING

FISHING LOG

LOG #

DATE

FISHING COMPANIONS

LOCATION

OBSERVATIONS

HIGHLIGHTS

WEATHER _____ **MOON PHASE** _____

AIR TEMPERATURE _____ **WATER TEMPERATURE** _____

WIND SPEED/DIRECTION _____

WATER CONDITIONS (level, clarity) _____

EQUIPMENT USED _____

CATCHLIST				
SPECIES	LENGTH / WEIGHT	BAIT/LURE/FLY	OTHER TACKLE	TIME

OVERALL RATING

FISHING LOG

LOG #

DATE

FISHING COMPANIONS

LOCATION

OBSERVATIONS

HIGHLIGHTS

WEATHER _____ MOON PHASE _____

AIR TEMPERATURE _____ WATER TEMPERATURE _____

WIND SPEED/DIRECTION _____

WATER CONDITIONS (level, clarity) _____

EQUIPMENT USED _____

CATCHLIST				
SPECIES	LENGTH / WEIGHT	BAIT/LURE/FLY	OTHER TACKLE	TIME

OVERALL RATING ▸◂ ▸◂ ▸◂ ▸◂ ▸◂

FISHING LOG

LOG #

DATE

FISHING COMPANIONS

LOCATION

OBSERVATIONS

HIGHLIGHTS

WEATHER _____ MOON PHASE _____

AIR TEMPERATURE _____ WATER TEMPERATURE _____

WIND SPEED/DIRECTION _____

WATER CONDITIONS (level, clarity) _____

EQUIPMENT USED _____

CATCHLIST				
SPECIES	LENGTH / WEIGHT	BAIT/LURE/FLY	OTHER TACKLE	TIME

OVERALL RATING 🐟 🐟 🐟 🐟 🐟

FISHING LOG

LOG #

DATE

FISHING COMPANIONS

LOCATION

OBSERVATIONS

HIGHLIGHTS

WEATHER _____ MOON PHASE _____

AIR TEMPERATURE _____ WATER TEMPERATURE _____

WIND SPEED/DIRECTION _____

WATER CONDITIONS (level, clarity) _____

EQUIPMENT USED _____

CATCHLIST

SPECIES	LENGTH / WEIGHT	BAIT/LURE/FLY	OTHER TACKLE	TIME

OVERALL RATING

FISHING LOG

LOG #

DATE

FISHING COMPANIONS

LOCATION

OBSERVATIONS

HIGHLIGHTS

WEATHER _____ MOON PHASE _____

AIR TEMPERATURE _____ WATER TEMPERATURE _____

WIND SPEED/DIRECTION _____

WATER CONDITIONS (level, clarity) _____

EQUIPMENT USED _____

CATCHLIST				
SPECIES	LENGTH / WEIGHT	BAIT/LURE/FLY	OTHER TACKLE	TIME

OVERALL RATING

FISHING LOG

LOG #

DATE

FISHING COMPANIONS

LOCATION

OBSERVATIONS

HIGHLIGHTS

WEATHER _____ **MOON PHASE** _____

AIR TEMPERATURE _____ **WATER TEMPERATURE** _____

WIND SPEED/DIRECTION _____

WATER CONDITIONS (level, clarity) _____

EQUIPMENT USED _____

CATCHLIST				
SPECIES	LENGTH/WEIGHT	BAIT/LURE/FLY	OTHER TACKLE	TIME

OVERALL RATING

FISHING LOG

LOG #

DATE

FISHING COMPANIONS

LOCATION

OBSERVATIONS

_____

_____

_____

_____

_____

_____

_____

_____

_____

_____

_____

_____

_____

_____

_____

_____

_____

_____

HIGHLIGHTS

_____

_____

_____

_____

WEATHER _____ MOON PHASE _____

AIR TEMPERATURE _____ WATER TEMPERATURE _____

WIND SPEED/DIRECTION _____

WATER CONDITIONS (level, clarity) _____

EQUIPMENT USED _____

CATCHLIST				
SPECIES	LENGTH / WEIGHT	BAIT/LURE/FLY	OTHER TACKLE	TIME

OVERALL RATING 🐟 🐟 🐟 🐟 🐟

FISHING LOG

LOG #

DATE

FISHING COMPANIONS

LOCATION

OBSERVATIONS

HIGHLIGHTS

WEATHER _____ MOON PHASE _____

AIR TEMPERATURE _____ WATER TEMPERATURE _____

WIND SPEED/DIRECTION _____

WATER CONDITIONS (level, clarity) _____

EQUIPMENT USED _____

CATCHLIST				
SPECIES	LENGTH / WEIGHT	BAIT/LURE/FLY	OTHER TACKLE	TIME

OVERALL RATING

FISHING LOG

LOG #

DATE

FISHING COMPANIONS

LOCATION

OBSERVATIONS

HIGHLIGHTS

WEATHER _____ **MOON PHASE** _____

AIR TEMPERATURE _____ **WATER TEMPERATURE** _____

WIND SPEED/DIRECTION _____

WATER CONDITIONS (level, clarity) _____

EQUIPMENT USED _____

CATCHLIST				
SPECIES	LENGTH / WEIGHT	BAIT/LURE/FLY	OTHER TACKLE	TIME

OVERALL RATING

FISHING LOG

LOG #

DATE

FISHING COMPANIONS

LOCATION

OBSERVATIONS

HIGHLIGHTS

WEATHER _____ **MOON PHASE** _____

AIR TEMPERATURE _____ **WATER TEMPERATURE** _____

WIND SPEED/DIRECTION _____

WATER CONDITIONS (level, clarity) _____

EQUIPMENT USED _____

CATCHLIST				
SPECIES	LENGTH / WEIGHT	BAIT/LURE/FLY	OTHER TACKLE	TIME

OVERALL RATING 🐟 🐟 🐟 🐟 🐟

FISHING LOG

LOG #

DATE

FISHING COMPANIONS

LOCATION

OBSERVATIONS

HIGHLIGHTS

WEATHER _____ MOON PHASE _____

AIR TEMPERATURE _____ WATER TEMPERATURE _____

WIND SPEED/DIRECTION _____

WATER CONDITIONS (level, clarity) _____

EQUIPMENT USED _____

CATCHLIST				
SPECIES	LENGTH / WEIGHT	BAIT/LURE/FLY	OTHER TACKLE	TIME

OVERALL RATING

FISHING LOG

LOG #

DATE

FISHING COMPANIONS

LOCATION

OBSERVATIONS

HIGHLIGHTS

WEATHER _____ **MOON PHASE** _____

AIR TEMPERATURE _____ **WATER TEMPERATURE** _____

WIND SPEED/DIRECTION _____

WATER CONDITIONS (level, clarity) _____

EQUIPMENT USED _____

CATCHLIST				
SPECIES	LENGTH / WEIGHT	BAIT/LURE/FLY	OTHER TACKLE	TIME

OVERALL RATING

FISHING LOG

LOG #

DATE

FISHING COMPANIONS

LOCATION

OBSERVATIONS

_____
_____
_____
_____
_____
_____
_____
_____
_____
_____
_____
_____
_____
_____
_____
_____
_____
_____
_____

HIGHLIGHTS

_____
_____
_____

WEATHER _____ MOON PHASE _____

AIR TEMPERATURE _____ WATER TEMPERATURE _____

WIND SPEED/DIRECTION _____

WATER CONDITIONS (level, clarity) _____

EQUIPMENT USED _____

CATCHLIST				
SPECIES	LENGTH / WEIGHT	BAIT/LURE/FLY	OTHER TACKLE	TIME

OVERALL RATING 🐟 🐟 🐟 🐟 🐟

FISHING LOG

LOG #

DATE

FISHING COMPANIONS

LOCATION

OBSERVATIONS

HIGHLIGHTS

WEATHER _____ **MOON PHASE** _____

AIR TEMPERATURE _____ **WATER TEMPERATURE** _____

WIND SPEED/DIRECTION _____

WATER CONDITIONS (level, clarity) _____

EQUIPMENT USED _____

CATCHLIST				
SPECIES	LENGTH / WEIGHT	BAIT/LURE/FLY	OTHER TACKLE	TIME

OVERALL RATING 🐟 🐟 🐟 🐟 🐟

FISHING LOG

LOG #

DATE

FISHING COMPANIONS

LOCATION

OBSERVATIONS

_____

_____

_____

_____

_____

_____

_____

_____

_____

_____

_____

_____

_____

_____

_____

_____

_____

_____

_____

_____

HIGHLIGHTS

_____

_____

_____

WEATHER _____ **MOON PHASE** _____

AIR TEMPERATURE _____ **WATER TEMPERATURE** _____

WIND SPEED/DIRECTION _____

WATER CONDITIONS (level, clarity) _____

EQUIPMENT USED _____

CATCHLIST				
SPECIES	LENGTH / WEIGHT	BAIT/LURE/FLY	OTHER TACKLE	TIME

OVERALL RATING 🐟 🐟 🐟 🐟 🐟

FISHING LOG

LOG #

DATE

FISHING COMPANIONS

LOCATION

OBSERVATIONS

HIGHLIGHTS

WEATHER _____ MOON PHASE _____

AIR TEMPERATURE _____ WATER TEMPERATURE _____

WIND SPEED/DIRECTION _____

WATER CONDITIONS (level, clarity) _____

EQUIPMENT USED _____

CATCHLIST				
SPECIES	LENGTH / WEIGHT	BAIT/LURE/FLY	OTHER TACKLE	TIME

OVERALL RATING

FISHING LOG

LOG #

DATE

FISHING COMPANIONS

LOCATION

OBSERVATIONS

HIGHLIGHTS

WEATHER _____ MOON PHASE _____

AIR TEMPERATURE _____ WATER TEMPERATURE _____

WIND SPEED/DIRECTION _____

WATER CONDITIONS (level, clarity) _____

EQUIPMENT USED _____

CATCHLIST				
SPECIES	LENGTH / WEIGHT	BAIT/LURE/FLY	OTHER TACKLE	TIME

OVERALL RATING

FISHING LOG

LOG #

DATE

FISHING COMPANIONS

LOCATION

OBSERVATIONS

HIGHLIGHTS

WEATHER _____ **MOON PHASE** _____

AIR TEMPERATURE _____ **WATER TEMPERATURE** _____

WIND SPEED/DIRECTION _____

WATER CONDITIONS (level, clarity) _____

EQUIPMENT USED _____

CATCHLIST				
SPECIES	LENGTH / WEIGHT	BAIT/LURE/FLY	OTHER TACKLE	TIME

OVERALL RATING   ▶◀ ▶◀

FISHING LOG

LOG #

DATE

FISHING COMPANIONS

LOCATION

OBSERVATIONS

HIGHLIGHTS

WEATHER _____ MOON PHASE _____

AIR TEMPERATURE _____ WATER TEMPERATURE _____

WIND SPEED/DIRECTION _____

WATER CONDITIONS (level, clarity) _____

EQUIPMENT USED _____

CATCHLIST				
SPECIES	LENGTH / WEIGHT	BAIT/LURE/FLY	OTHER TACKLE	TIME

OVERALL RATING

FISHING LOG

LOG #

DATE

FISHING COMPANIONS

LOCATION

OBSERVATIONS

HIGHLIGHTS

WEATHER _____ **MOON PHASE** _____

AIR TEMPERATURE _____ **WATER TEMPERATURE** _____

WIND SPEED/DIRECTION _____

WATER CONDITIONS (level, clarity) _____

EQUIPMENT USED _____

CATCHLIST				
SPECIES	LENGTH / WEIGHT	BAIT/LURE/FLY	OTHER TACKLE	TIME

OVERALL RATING

FISHING LOG

LOG #

DATE

FISHING COMPANIONS

LOCATION

OBSERVATIONS

HIGHLIGHTS

WEATHER _____ **MOON PHASE** _____

AIR TEMPERATURE _____ **WATER TEMPERATURE** _____

WIND SPEED/DIRECTION _____

WATER CONDITIONS (level, clarity) _____

EQUIPMENT USED _____

CATCHLIST				
SPECIES	LENGTH / WEIGHT	BAIT/LURE/FLY	OTHER TACKLE	TIME

OVERALL RATING

FISHING LOG

LOG #

DATE

FISHING COMPANIONS

LOCATION

OBSERVATIONS

HIGHLIGHTS

WEATHER ———————————— **MOON PHASE** —————————

AIR TEMPERATURE ————————— **WATER TEMPERATURE** ——————

WIND SPEED/DIRECTION ————————————————————

WATER CONDITIONS (level, clarity) ——————————————————

EQUIPMENT USED ———————————————————————

CATCHLIST				
SPECIES	LENGTH / WEIGHT	BAIT/LURE/FLY	OTHER TACKLE	TIME

OVERALL RATING

FISHING LOG

LOG #

DATE

FISHING COMPANIONS

LOCATION

OBSERVATIONS

HIGHLIGHTS

WEATHER _____ **MOON PHASE** _____

AIR TEMPERATURE _____ **WATER TEMPERATURE** _____

WIND SPEED/DIRECTION _____

WATER CONDITIONS (level, clarity) _____

EQUIPMENT USED _____

CATCHLIST				
SPECIES	**LENGTH / WEIGHT**	**BAIT/LURE/FLY**	**OTHER TACKLE**	**TIME**

OVERALL RATING

FISHING LOG

LOG #

DATE

FISHING COMPANIONS

LOCATION

OBSERVATIONS

HIGHLIGHTS

WEATHER _____ MOON PHASE _____

AIR TEMPERATURE _____ WATER TEMPERATURE _____

WIND SPEED/DIRECTION _____

WATER CONDITIONS (level, clarity) _____

EQUIPMENT USED _____

CATCHLIST				
SPECIES	LENGTH / WEIGHT	BAIT/LURE/FLY	OTHER TACKLE	TIME

OVERALL RATING

FISHING LOG

LOG #

DATE

FISHING COMPANIONS

LOCATION

OBSERVATIONS

HIGHLIGHTS

WEATHER _____ MOON PHASE _____

AIR TEMPERATURE _____ WATER TEMPERATURE _____

WIND SPEED/DIRECTION _____

WATER CONDITIONS (level, clarity) _____

EQUIPMENT USED _____

CATCHLIST				
SPECIES	LENGTH / WEIGHT	BAIT/LURE/FLY	OTHER TACKLE	TIME

OVERALL RATING

FISHING LOG

LOG #

DATE

FISHING COMPANIONS

LOCATION

OBSERVATIONS

HIGHLIGHTS

WEATHER _____ MOON PHASE _____

AIR TEMPERATURE _____ WATER TEMPERATURE _____

WIND SPEED/DIRECTION _____

WATER CONDITIONS (level, clarity) _____

EQUIPMENT USED _____

CATCHLIST				
SPECIES	LENGTH / WEIGHT	BAIT/LURE/FLY	OTHER TACKLE	TIME

OVERALL RATING ▸▰▸ ▸▰▸ ▸▰▸ ▸▰▸ ▸▰▸

FISHING LOG

LOG #

DATE

FISHING COMPANIONS

LOCATION

OBSERVATIONS

HIGHLIGHTS

WEATHER _____ **MOON PHASE** _____

AIR TEMPERATURE _____ **WATER TEMPERATURE** _____

WIND SPEED/DIRECTION _____

WATER CONDITIONS (level, clarity) _____

EQUIPMENT USED _____

CATCHLIST				
SPECIES	LENGTH / WEIGHT	BAIT/LURE/FLY	OTHER TACKLE	TIME

OVERALL RATING 🐟 🐟 🐟 🐟 🐟

FISHING LOG

LOG #

DATE

FISHING COMPANIONS

LOCATION

OBSERVATIONS _____

_____

_____

_____

_____

_____

_____

_____

_____

_____

_____

_____

_____

_____

_____

_____

_____

_____

_____

_____

HIGHLIGHTS _____

_____

_____

_____

WEATHER _____   MOON PHASE _____

AIR TEMPERATURE _____   WATER TEMPERATURE _____

WIND SPEED/DIRECTION _____

WATER CONDITIONS (level, clarity) _____

EQUIPMENT USED _____

CATCHLIST				
SPECIES	LENGTH / WEIGHT	BAIT/LURE/FLY	OTHER TACKLE	TIME

OVERALL RATING 🐟 🐟 🐟 🐟 🐟

FISHING LOG

LOG #

DATE

FISHING COMPANIONS

LOCATION

OBSERVATIONS

HIGHLIGHTS

WEATHER _____ MOON PHASE _____

AIR TEMPERATURE _____ WATER TEMPERATURE _____

WIND SPEED/DIRECTION _____

WATER CONDITIONS (level, clarity) _____

EQUIPMENT USED _____

CATCHLIST				
SPECIES	LENGTH / WEIGHT	BAIT/LURE/FLY	OTHER TACKLE	TIME

OVERALL RATING

FISHING LOG

LOG #

DATE

FISHING COMPANIONS

LOCATION

OBSERVATIONS

HIGHLIGHTS

WEATHER _____ MOON PHASE _____

AIR TEMPERATURE _____ WATER TEMPERATURE _____

WIND SPEED/DIRECTION _____

WATER CONDITIONS (level, clarity) _____

EQUIPMENT USED _____

CATCHLIST				
SPECIES	LENGTH / WEIGHT	BAIT / LURE / FLY	OTHER TACKLE	TIME

OVERALL RATING

FISHING LOG

LOG #

DATE

FISHING COMPANIONS

LOCATION

OBSERVATIONS

_____
_____
_____
_____
_____
_____
_____
_____
_____
_____
_____
_____
_____
_____
_____
_____
_____
_____
_____

HIGHLIGHTS

_____
_____
_____

WEATHER _____   MOON PHASE _____

AIR TEMPERATURE _____   WATER TEMPERATURE _____

WIND SPEED/DIRECTION _____

WATER CONDITIONS (level, clarity) _____

EQUIPMENT USED _____

CATCHLIST				
SPECIES	LENGTH / WEIGHT	BAIT/LURE/FLY	OTHER TACKLE	TIME

OVERALL RATING 🐟 🐟 🐟 🐟 🐟

FISHING LOG

LOG #

DATE

FISHING COMPANIONS

LOCATION

OBSERVATIONS

HIGHLIGHTS

WEATHER _____ MOON PHASE _____

AIR TEMPERATURE _____ WATER TEMPERATURE _____

WIND SPEED/DIRECTION _____

WATER CONDITIONS (level, clarity) _____

EQUIPMENT USED _____

CATCHLIST				
SPECIES	LENGTH / WEIGHT	BAIT/LURE/FLY	OTHER TACKLE	TIME

OVERALL RATING 🐟 🐟 🐟 🐟 🐟

FISHING LOG

LOG #

DATE

FISHING COMPANIONS

LOCATION

OBSERVATIONS

HIGHLIGHTS

WEATHER _____ MOON PHASE _____

AIR TEMPERATURE _____ WATER TEMPERATURE _____

WIND SPEED/DIRECTION _____

WATER CONDITIONS (level, clarity) _____

EQUIPMENT USED _____

CATCHLIST				
SPECIES	LENGTH / WEIGHT	BAIT/LURE/FLY	OTHER TACKLE	TIME

OVERALL RATING

FISHING LOG

LOG #

DATE

FISHING COMPANIONS

LOCATION

OBSERVATIONS

HIGHLIGHTS

WEATHER _____ MOON PHASE _____

AIR TEMPERATURE _____ WATER TEMPERATURE _____

WIND SPEED/DIRECTION _____

WATER CONDITIONS (level, clarity) _____

EQUIPMENT USED _____

CATCHLIST				
SPECIES	LENGTH / WEIGHT	BAIT/LURE/FLY	OTHER TACKLE	TIME

OVERALL RATING 

FISHING LOG

LOG #

DATE

FISHING COMPANIONS

LOCATION

OBSERVATIONS

HIGHLIGHTS

WEATHER _____ MOON PHASE _____

AIR TEMPERATURE _____ WATER TEMPERATURE _____

WIND SPEED/DIRECTION _____

WATER CONDITIONS (level, clarity) _____

EQUIPMENT USED _____

CATCHLIST				
SPECIES	LENGTH / WEIGHT	BAIT/LURE/FLY	OTHER TACKLE	TIME

OVERALL RATING

FISHING LOG

LOG #

DATE

FISHING COMPANIONS

LOCATION

OBSERVATIONS

HIGHLIGHTS

WEATHER _____ **MOON PHASE** _____

AIR TEMPERATURE _____ **WATER TEMPERATURE** _____

WIND SPEED/DIRECTION _____

WATER CONDITIONS (level, clarity) _____

EQUIPMENT USED _____

CATCHLIST				
SPECIES	LENGTH / WEIGHT	BAIT/LURE/FLY	OTHER TACKLE	TIME

OVERALL RATING   🐟 🐟 🐟 🐟 🐟

FISHING LOG

LOG #

DATE

FISHING COMPANIONS

LOCATION

OBSERVATIONS

HIGHLIGHTS

WEATHER _____ MOON PHASE _____

AIR TEMPERATURE _____ WATER TEMPERATURE _____

WIND SPEED/DIRECTION _____

WATER CONDITIONS (level, clarity) _____

EQUIPMENT USED _____

CATCHLIST				
SPECIES	LENGTH / WEIGHT	BAIT/LURE/FLY	OTHER TACKLE	TIME

OVERALL RATING 🐟 🐟 🐟 🐟 🐟

FISHING LOG

LOG #

DATE

FISHING COMPANIONS

LOCATION

OBSERVATIONS

HIGHLIGHTS

WEATHER _____ MOON PHASE _____

AIR TEMPERATURE _____ WATER TEMPERATURE _____

WIND SPEED/DIRECTION _____

WATER CONDITIONS (level, clarity) _____

EQUIPMENT USED _____

CATCHLIST				
SPECIES	LENGTH / WEIGHT	BAIT/LURE/FLY	OTHER TACKLE	TIME

OVERALL RATING

FISHING LOG

LOG #

DATE

FISHING COMPANIONS

LOCATION

OBSERVATIONS

HIGHLIGHTS

WEATHER _____ MOON PHASE _____

AIR TEMPERATURE _____ WATER TEMPERATURE _____

WIND SPEED/DIRECTION _____

WATER CONDITIONS (level, clarity) _____

EQUIPMENT USED _____

CATCHLIST				
SPECIES	LENGTH / WEIGHT	BAIT/LURE/FLY	OTHER TACKLE	TIME

OVERALL RATING

NOTES & SKETCHES

"IF PEOPLE CONCENTRATED ON THE REALLY IMPORTANT THINGS IN LIFE, THERE'D BE A SHORTAGE OF FISHING POLES."

—Doug Larson

"I'VE SPENT AS MUCH OF MY LIFE FISHING AS DECENCY ALLOWED, AND SOMETIMES I DON'T LET EVEN THAT GET IN MY WAY."

—Thomas McGuane

"THE CHARM OF FISHING IS THAT IT IS THE PURSUIT OF WHAT IS ELUSIVE
BUT ATTAINABLE, A PERPETUAL SERIES OF OCCASIONS OF HOPE."

—John Buchan

"I LOVE FISHING. YOU PUT THAT LINE IN THE WATER
AND YOU DON'T KNOW WHAT'S ON THE OTHER END.
YOUR IMAGINATION IS UNDER THERE."
—Robert Altman

"THERE IS CERTAINLY SOMETHING IN ANGLING THAT TENDS
TO PRODUCE A SERENITY OF THE MIND."

—Washington Irving

"THERE ARE ALWAYS NEW PLACES TO GO FISHING.
FOR ANY FISHERMAN, THERE'S ALWAYS A NEW PLACE,
ALWAYS A NEW HORIZON."

—Jack Nicklaus

"FISHING IS NOT AN ESCAPE FROM LIFE,
BUT OFTEN A DEEPER IMMERSION INTO IT."

—Harry Middleton

"FISHING IS MARVELOUS . . . THERE IS THE IRRESISTIBLE URGE TO TANGLE WITH THE MYSTERIOUS AND UNKNOWN, TO RELY ON INTUITION AND HUNCHES."

—Katharine Weber

"I'VE GONE FISHING THOUSANDS OF TIMES IN MY LIFE, AND I HAVE NEVER ONCE FELT UNLUCKY OR POORLY PAID FOR THOSE HOURS ON THE WATER."

—William Tapply

"IT IS IMPOSSIBLE TO GROW WEARY OF A SPORT THAT IS
NEVER THE SAME ON ANY TWO DAYS OF THE YEAR."

—Theodore Gordon

FISHING CHECKLISTS

MY ALL-TIME FAVORITE FISHING TRIPS

DON'T LET TIME ERASE the memory of your best fishing spots and most impressive catches. Keep track of your truly unforgettable fishing trips here.

DATE

LOCATION

HIGHLIGHTS _____

_____

_____

_____

_____

_____

DATE

LOCATION

HIGHLIGHTS _____

_____

_____

_____

_____

DATE   **LOCATION**

HIGHLIGHTS _____
_____
_____
_____
_____
_____

DATE   **LOCATION**

HIGHLIGHTS _____
_____
_____
_____
_____
_____

DATE   **LOCATION**

HIGHLIGHTS _____
_____
_____
_____
_____
_____

MY ALL-TIME FAVORITE FISHING TRIPS

DATE

LOCATION

HIGHLIGHTS _____

_____

_____

_____

_____

_____

DATE

LOCATION

HIGHLIGHTS _____

_____

_____

_____

_____

_____

DATE

LOCATION

HIGHLIGHTS _____

_____

_____

_____

_____

MY ALL-TIME FAVORITE FISHING TRIPS

DATE

LOCATION

HIGHLIGHTS _____
_____
_____
_____
_____
_____

DATE

LOCATION

HIGHLIGHTS _____
_____
_____
_____
_____
_____

DATE

LOCATION

HIGHLIGHTS _____
_____
_____
_____
_____

MY FISHING BUCKET LIST

HERE'S WHERE YOU CAN RECORD your wildest fishing dreams: places you'd like to visit, fish you'd like to catch, or gear you'd like to try out. Once you've actually done the things you list here, just check them off and bask in the glory.

- [ ] _____
- [ ] _____
- [ ] _____
- [ ] _____
- [ ] _____
- [ ] _____
- [ ] _____
- [ ] _____
- [ ] _____
- [ ] _____
- [ ] _____
- [ ] _____
- [ ] _____
- [ ] _____
- [ ] _____
- [ ] _____
- [ ] _____
- [ ] _____
- [ ] _____

FISH I'VE CAUGHT

ON THE NEXT FOUR PAGES, keep a record of first-time catches or particularly memorable fish and the days you caught them.

SPECIES	SPECIES	DATE CAUGHT
SPECIES	SPECIES	DATE CAUGHT
SPECIES	SPECIES	DATE CAUGHT
SPECIES	SPECIES	DATE CAUGHT
SPECIES	SPECIES	DATE CAUGHT
SPECIES	SPECIES	DATE CAUGHT
SPECIES	SPECIES	DATE CAUGHT
SPECIES	SPECIES	DATE CAUGHT
SPECIES	SPECIES	DATE CAUGHT

FISH I'VE CAUGHT

SPECIES	DATE CAUGHT
SPECIES	DATE CAUGHT
SPECIES	DATE CAUGHT
SPECIES	DATE CAUGHT
SPECIES	DATE CAUGHT
SPECIES	DATE CAUGHT
SPECIES	DATE CAUGHT
SPECIES	DATE CAUGHT
SPECIES	DATE CAUGHT
SPECIES	DATE CAUGHT
SPECIES	DATE CAUGHT

FISH I'VE CAUGHT

SPECIES	DATE CAUGHT
SPECIES	DATE CAUGHT
SPECIES	DATE CAUGHT
SPECIES	DATE CAUGHT
SPECIES	DATE CAUGHT
SPECIES	DATE CAUGHT
SPECIES	DATE CAUGHT
SPECIES	DATE CAUGHT
SPECIES	DATE CAUGHT
SPECIES	DATE CAUGHT
SPECIES	DATE CAUGHT

FISH I'VE CAUGHT

SPECIES	DATE CAUGHT
SPECIES	DATE CAUGHT
SPECIES	DATE CAUGHT
SPECIES	DATE CAUGHT
SPECIES	DATE CAUGHT
SPECIES	DATE CAUGHT
SPECIES	DATE CAUGHT
SPECIES	DATE CAUGHT
SPECIES	DATE CAUGHT
SPECIES	DATE CAUGHT
SPECIES	DATE CAUGHT

THE
FISHERMAN'S

JOURNAL

weldon**owen**

www.weldonowen.com

ISBN 978-1-68188-645-9

PRINTED IN CHINA

10 9 8 7 6 5 4 3 2 1